Fabulously Fierce

"When going after what you really want, fiercely walk in authority!"

Dr. Deborah Allen

Celebrating release of: FABULOUSLY FIERCE EAU DE PARFUM ~ DEBORAH ALLEN COLLECTION

© 2023 Dr. Deborah Allen

Book Cover & Interior Design: Nichol LeAnn Perricci

ALL RIGHTS RESERVED. No part of this book may be reproduced in any written, electronic, recording, or photocopying without written permission of the publisher or author. The exception would be in the case of brief quotations embodied in critical articles or reviews and pages where permission is specifically granted by the publisher or author.

LEGAL DISCLAIMER. Although the author has made every effort to ensure that the information in this book was correct at press time, the author does not assume hereby disclaim any liability to any party for loss, damage, or disruption caused by errors or missions, whether such errors or omissions result from negligence, accident, or any other cause.

Published By: Igniting the Flame Publishing

Library of Congress Cataloging-in-Publication Data has been applied for.

ISBN: 9798387533266

PRINTED IN THE UNITED STATES OF AMERICA

Fabulously Fierce

For Apostle Dr. Glen Allen Sr, who believed in & saw the fierceness in me! Also written for every one that has felt like they could never get back up. It is possible not only to get up but get up and dream on a larger level. Fabulously Fierce was something spoken into my vision that caused the baby in my womb to leap! It's time for you to take your power back and go after what you really want.

"When walking in purpose, fiercely walk in divine authority!"

Apostle Dr. Deborah Allen

Dr. Deborah Allen

Contents

Foreword .... Page 5

From the Author .... Page 7

Acknowledgments .... Page 11

Introduction .... Page 13

Chapter 1: F – Find yourself .... Page 15

Chapter 2: I – Indeed be independent .... Page 24

Chapter 3: E- Evaluate your life & story .... Page 32

Chapter 4: R – Realize you make the difference .... Pg 41

Chapter 5: C – Create your opportunity through purpose ... Pg 49

Chapter 6: E – Evolve into the greatest version of you .... Pg 58

Chapter 7 - Fiercely walk in authority .... Page 67

Fierce System Recap .... Page 75

About the Perfume .... Page 77

About the Author .... Page 84

Foreword

It is my great pleasure to introduce you to the captivating world of Fabulously Fierce, a new fragrance created by the talented and innovative Dr. Deborah Allen. As you embark on this olfactory journey, the companion book of the same name will guide you through the beauty and essence of this luxurious fragrance.

Fabulously Fierce is not just a perfume, it is a statement. It is a symbol of empowerment, of confidence, and of unapologetic boldness. From the first spritz to the final notes, this scent will transport you to a world of glamour, sophistication, and sensuality.

But the experience of Fabulously Fierce goes beyond just the fragrance itself. This companion book will take you on a journey of discovery, exploring the inspiration, ingredients, and intricate details that make this scent truly extraordinary.

Each page is exquisitely crafted to reflect the essence of the fragrance and its unique personality.

With each turn of the page, you will uncover the carefully selected notes that make up this luxurious scent - from the spicy warmth of pink pepper to the rich, indulgent aroma of amber. Dr. Deborah Allen's attention to detail and her passion for excellence shines through every word, capturing the essence of the fragrance in all its glory.

So, whether you are a connoisseur of fine fragrances or simply someone who appreciates the finer things in life, Fabulously Fierce will captivate you from start to finish. It is my honor to introduce you to this exquisite fragrance and its companion book, and I hope you will enjoy this journey of discovery as much as I have.

Dr. Jacquie Hadnot,
Author, Perfumer & Entrepreneur

jacquie@jacquiehadnot.com
www.jacquiehadnot.com
www.malieboushaye.com

From the Author

Fabulously Fierce perfume was created and birthed because I refused to stay down. It's the result of bossing back up and taking back the strength of my own destiny. I'm so honored to share a tool or rather system that propelled me into action. I am Deborah Allen the creator of "The FIERCE System". My one and only goal is to inspire others and assist them in creating the life that they were meant to live. The journey towards achieving what you truly desire may not always be easy, but it's always worth every battle and sacrifice. Living through the process of becoming the greatest version of oneself is a transformative journey that can be both challenging and rewarding. It's a journey that requires courage, determination, strength and a belief in oneself. So, believe in you again! We have entered in a time of dreaming and birthing those dreams, healthy and whole.

Yes, self-growth is a choice. It happens by building, investing, and betting on you! There must be a change in how we see ourselves and what's happening around us. Not only that it's influenced by the story we tell ourselves and others. It is important that we all program ourselves to grow, advance, excel and win. This book is birth from the place of great stretching in my life. Fabulously Fierce is written in honor and celebration of the release and celebration of this extraordinary perfume line. Fabulously Fierce ~ April 2023

DEBORAH ALLEN COLLECTION
FABULOUSLY FIERCE EAU DE PARFUM

Indulge in the sultry and seductive aroma of ***Fabulously Fierce Eau De Parfum*** from the Deborah Allen Collection.

This exotic fragrance transports you to a world of sensuality and mystique, with its vibrant blend of top notes including zesty Orange Blossom, juicy Brazilian Cherry, and luscious Fresh Raspberry. The sharp and invigorating notes of Petitgrain, Cardamom and Bergamot add a touch of mystery and intrigue, evoking an air of daring adventure.

Fabulously Fierce

As the fragrance settles, the heart notes of Orange Hibiscus, Lily-of-the-Valley, Jasmine, and Sage reveal themselves in a harmonious and intoxicating melody. These floral and herbal notes create a captivating and alluring aura, tempting the senses and heightening your desire.

The fragrance lingers with its unforgettable base notes of warm Amber, rich Musk, and smooth Sandalwood. These luxurious and seductive scents create a hypnotic and irresistible trail, leaving you feeling empowered and confident, ready to conquer the world.

Fabulously Fierce Eau De Parfum from the Deborah Allen Collection is the perfect fragrance for those who embrace their sensuality and exude an air of unapologetic confidence. It is a scent that will captivate and enchant those around you, leaving them in awe of your sheer power and magnetism.

Dr. Deborah Allen

Acknowledgments

Fabulously Fierce is the result of me being fierce and becoming the women I was always destined to be. It became possible through sharing my voice and silencing fear. This book is a great testament of the movement, that my first book "Fierce" has brought on a global level. That book truly birthed forth great destiny, vision and purpose in my life and the lives of many. Truly I am honored and grateful for all the support and love that has been shown unto me over the years. Understand and know I am forever grateful!

I serve in ministry with a mighty man of valor, Apostle Dr. Glen Allen Sr. We have served happily and strategically now for over 23 years. Lighthouse Apostolic Ministries of God Church thank you for being a mighty team and a place of vision. Lighthouse we be mighty!

Amazingly, I have been allowed to birth six children but be the mother of nine. Our children have been a blessing to my very existence. I'm so awed by the support that I have received from family, friends, saints and clients over the years. Your love has been priceless. You have been my "why" and necessary for the shift that took place inside of me.

Introduction

Fabulously Fierce perfume line is not just a fragrance, it's a symbol of my unwavering passion and commitment to creating something truly remarkable that embodies the essence of empowerment and inspires everyone to unleash their inner fierceness.

When going after what you really want your mindset is everything. What you focus on will be what you bring to fruition. I was born to be an entrepreneur and champion. So, too are you born to excel. This system is an amazing tool that you can use to have growth, self-development and even reinvent your-self. The goal of this book for you to become fierce in your pursuit to win even fulfil your purpose. Through this system we will be strong and preserver toward your destiny. Understand that it takes grit to win. It is our time to walk fiercely in destiny and authority in life. This is a book that will lift, inspire, liberate and motivate you no matter what season in life you are in. This book will talk to you even shift you into your next or new level. You are fierce and built to last.

When you have a clear vision of what you want to achieve, it's important to believe in yourself and your abilities. Walking in authority means taking ownership of your goals and approaching them with confidence and determination. Remember, the path to success may not always be easy, but with a fierce attitude and unwavering commitment, you have the power to overcome any obstacles that come your way. So go after what you really want with all your heart and soul and let your authority that you walk in guide you towards your dreams!

Chapter 1:
Find yourself...

"To find yourself, think for yourself." – Socrates

Boom, Socrates is so on point with that quote! Just one quote can change your entire perception! Finding your authentic voice also is a key to unlocking your next level. Permission is not needed for you to thrive and launch forward on another level. Access has been granted to you to think about your own dreams, goals and developing of you. It's high time for you to be true to who you are at your core. Understand how very precious you are. Do not be a copycat or counterfeit in this dispensation. Being authentic compels, sells, and attract people to you. We cannot be whole or something to somebody else when we are not true to ourselves. It is not selfish to think about your own future. However, it is a requirement to reinvent yourself.

Finding yourself is a journey of self-discovery that can lead to a more meaningful and fulfilling life. It requires introspection, self-awareness, and a willingness to explore the depths of one's being. When you find yourself, you gain a sense of clarity about who you are, what you stand for, and what you want in life. You become more confident, self-assured, and purposeful in your actions.

The process of finding yourself is not always easy. It can involve facing your fears, challenging your beliefs, and stepping out of your comfort zone. But the rewards are worth it. When you find yourself, you tap into your true potential and unlock a sense of purpose that can propel you towards success and happiness.

The journey of finding yourself is unique to each individual. There is no one-size-fits-all approach, and the path can be filled with twists and turns. But with determination and a commitment to personal growth, anyone can embark on this transformative journey and discover their true self. Don't be afraid to start the journey of finding yourself. It may take time and effort, but the result is a life that is truly your own, lived on your terms, and guided by your innermost desires and values. Finding yourself allows you to take the greatest steps than you ever imagine. It is not over for you for you are still alive & breathing. Do not play it safe but be radical & find the fierce you again!

Fabulously Fierce

Journal ~ Find You.

Dr. Deborah Allen

Fabulously Fierce

Dr. Deborah Allen

Fabulously Fierce

Dr. Deborah Allen

Chapter 2:

Indeed be independent...

"Embrace your independence and go after what you want." - Kaitlyn Kaerhart

Woo-hoo! What you think or believe about yourself is so much more relevant than what others think about you. Indeed, be independent (freedom from the control, influence, support, aid, or the like, of others) and take your power back. The most powerful and courageous thing is to think for yourself and indeed be independent. Your mind opens limitless possibilities just for you. You are the major decision maker for you and hold power in your own hands. Be independent because you have control over your own destiny. Being independent in your life means taking control of your own destiny and making your own decisions without relying on others to guide or support you. It empowers you to create the life you want, based on your own values and goals. Independence allows you to stand on your own two feet, to be self-sufficient, and to face challenges with confidence and resilience. It frees you from the limitations of relying on others and enables you to forge your own path towards success and fulfillment. Ultimately, being independent is a powerful way to live your life on your own terms and to become the best version of yourself.

Be independent because doing what you love changes your attitude and flow of your entire life. It allows you to explore and puts the pep back in your steps. Also it gives you a new lease on life when you are doing what you or meant to do. Truly it is time for you to be independent and do the work. You can have what you have always seen in your dreams and to bring your goals to pass. Be strong, stand and be you. Come from under the corporate thumb & any mindset that limits you. Stay free & independent. Enlarge your territories and live on another level. Be independent spread your wings and fly.

Fabulously Fierce

Journal ~ Indeed be independent.

Dr. Deborah Allen

Fabulously Fierce

Dr. Deborah Allen

Fabulously Fierce

Dr. Deborah Allen

Chapter 3: Evaluate your life & story...

All I can do is make the best of what I am, become accustomed to it, evaluate the possibilities, and take advantage of them the best I can." - Jean-Paul Sartre

Yes, truly there is some truth in this quote that I can evaluate and take advantage of what I have lived and learned. Learning from our past impacts the projection of our future! History reveals some powerful keys about living and universal laws. It is vital that you evaluate your life and story with the clear eyes of wisdom of being an adult. Look at your life story from the mindset of the mature you and not the broken or fearful child you were of the past.

Evaluating your life and story can be a powerful motivator to help you achieve your goals and live a more fulfilling life. By taking a step back and reflecting on your experiences, you can gain valuable insights into what has worked well for you, as well as areas where you can improve.

Remember, your life is a unique story that only you can write. You have the power to shape your future, and every experience you had, whether good or bad, is an opportunity to learn, grow, and become a better version of you.

So, take the time to evaluate your life and story. Celebrate your successes, learn from your mistakes, and use your insights to chart a course towards a brighter future. Remember that your story is still being written, and with dedication, hard work, and perseverance, you have the power to create a life that is truly extraordinary. Look back at your life and your story will be powerful because how far you have come. Make every tear, trial, setback even pain count for a higher good. Understand that fear and doubt or nothing but bullying winds you can overthrow. Nothing can hinder you sharing your phenomenal story that you have evaluated and grew from. Now use that insight to change the world with it!

Dr. Deborah Allen

Journal ~ Evaluate your life & story.

Fabulously Fierce

Dr. Deborah Allen

Fabulously Fierce

Dr. Deborah Allen

Fabulously Fierce

Chapter 4:
Realize you make the difference...

Great leaders don't set out to be a leader, they set out to make a difference. It's never about the role, always about the goal. – **Jeremy Bravo**

Wow, realize you make the difference even if you were born from a mistake, mishap, rape, incest, on an abandoned floor or even if you were put up for adoption. I am charging everyone that read this book to realize you make the difference and work what you have in your hand to succeed. Everyone can do simple things to make a difference but realize you make the ultimate difference. It's easy to feel small and insignificant in a world that can often feel overwhelming and chaotic. But the truth is, every action you take, every decision you make, has the power to make a difference.

Fabulously Fierce

Whether it's something as small as a kind word or gesture, or something as big as starting a movement to change the world, every act of kindness, compassion, and determination has the power to create a ripple effect that can change the course of history.

So, don't underestimate the power of your actions. Realize that you make the difference and use that knowledge to fuel your passion and drive to achieve your goals and make the world a better place. Remember that even the smallest actions can have a profound impact, and that by working together, we can create a brighter, more compassionate, and more just world for all. Realize you make the difference so roar, hunt and enlarge your territory. Elite people are called to walk to a different drummer. You have been born to shift everything around you and connected to you. So, rob the cemetery of the gift of your voice.

Dr. Deborah Allen

Journal ~ Realize you make the difference.

Fabulously Fierce

Dr. Deborah Allen

Fabulously Fierce

Dr. Deborah Allen

Fabulously Fierce

Chapter 5: Create your opportunity through purpose...

"Your big opportunity may be right where you are now."
- Napoleon Hill

Tadah, your opportunity can be right where you are at now but make them if they are not! Ultimately, you make your own luck so let us get in boss/beast mode. It's time to pursue your dreams and goals and they are reachable if only you believe. Be a person of focus, hopefulness, and determination. Come on Bosses and let us boss up or better yet level up. Create your opportunity through purpose is intentional. Success comes through planning not just by wishing. You cannot just throw something at the wall and hope it sticks. No, yet you must and can create opportunities from your purpose. Creating your opportunity through purpose is a powerful way to take control of your life and shape your own destiny. When you have a clear sense of purpose, you can use it as a guiding light to help you identify opportunities that align with your values, passions, and goals.

By staying true to your purpose, you can create a vision for your life that is meaningful, fulfilling, and purposeful. You can leverage your unique strengths and talents to make a positive impact in the world, and to create opportunities for yourself that may not have otherwise existed.

When you have a strong sense of purpose, you can approach challenges with confidence and resilience. You can use setbacks as opportunities to learn, grow, and refine your vision for the future. And you can inspire others to join you on your journey, creating a community of like-minded individuals who are committed to creating a better world.

So, if you want to create your own opportunities, start by identifying your purpose.

Cultivate a deep sense of meaning and fulfillment in your life and let that guide you towards the opportunities that are right for you. Remember, you have the power to shape your own destiny and create a life that is truly extraordinary. We are great thinkers and it's why we keep pushing our purpose. By creating opportunities through purpose, we are shattering the glass ceiling and stepping into the impossible,

Fabulously Fierce

Journal ~ Create your opportunity through purpose.

Dr. Deborah Allen

Fabulously Fierce

Fabulously Fierce

Dr. Deborah Allen

Chapter 6: Evolve into the greatest version of you...

"Make the most of yourself for that is all there is of you." — *Ralph Waldo Emerson*

Greatness is pulling you to be the best version that you can and ever have been. Alright, you must evolve into that greatest version of you doing this season of manifestation. Nothing in life stays the same and neither should you. Time does and should bring a better change even growth into our lives and the world. Change who you are to become who you are meant to forever be. The definition of evolve is develop gradually, especially from a simple to a more complex form. Evolve into the greatest version of you. Fierceness is embedded into your core and allows you to endure all the inner work it takes to evolve. You have the ability tom evolve, go through and shift like a superhero. You will not be defeated!

Not only that but you are so motivated & focused to win. Maturity and purging of your mind are a mandatory step in evolving. No longer can the child mindset stay but the adult you must emerge the victor. Be strong in mind, thought, dreams and goals.

Evolution is a constant process, and it applies not only to living beings but also to our personal growth and development. Each one of us has the potential to evolve into the greatest version of ourselves, but it requires dedication, self-awareness, and a willingness to step outside our comfort zone. Remember, your greatest version is not a destination, but a journey. Every day, strive to become a little bit better than you were yesterday. Embrace your strengths, work on your weaknesses, and don't be afraid to take risks and try new things.

As you evolve, you'll discover new passions, unlock hidden talents, and develop a deeper sense of purpose and fulfillment. The journey may not always be easy, but the rewards are immeasurable.

So, embrace the journey, trust the process, and evolve into the greatest version of yourself. You are capable of tremendous things! We have done more than survived and it has cause us to be evolved.

Dr. Deborah Allen

Journal ~ Evolve into the greatest version of you.

Fabulously Fierce

Dr. Deborah Allen

Fabulously Fierce

Dr. Deborah Allen

Fabulously Fierce

Chapter 7: Fiercely walk in authority...

His authority on earth allows us to dare to go to all the nations. His authority in heaven gives us our only hope of success. And His presence with us leaves us no other choice. - John Stott

Be fierce and stand in God! Walking in authority means having a deep understanding of your value, purpose, and strengths, and fearlessly living out your truth. It means standing firm in your beliefs, and confidently asserting your power and influence in any situation.

Fiercely walking in authority requires courage, self-awareness, and a strong sense of identity. It means taking ownership of your life and decisions, and not allowing external circumstances or opinions to define you.

When you walk in authority, you inspire others to do the same. You become a beacon of strength and confidence, and people look up to you for guidance and inspiration. You become a powerful force for positive change, both in your own life and in the lives of those around you. So, don't be afraid to step into your power, and fiercely walk in authority. You have the ability to make a difference and create the life you desire and born to live. Build the life and business you deeply desire by walking in your purpose. "When walking in purpose, fiercely walk in divine authority!"

Fabulously Fierce Eau De Parfum from the Deborah Allen Collection was just a whisper in my subconscious. This exotic fragrance transports you to a world of sensuality, mystique, adventure and unlimited possibilities.

The F.I.E.R.C.E. System stepped me into living one of the greatest movements of my life: The unveiling of Fabulously Fierce Eau De Parfum, April 14, 2023.

Dr. Deborah Allen

Journal ~ Fiercely walk in authority.

Fabulously Fierce

Dr. Deborah Allen

Fabulously Fierce

Dr. Deborah Allen

Fabulously Fierce

Dr. Deborah Allen

The Fierce System:

1. **F** – Find yourself...Find your true self and be true to your own voice, dreams, and goals.
2. **I** – Indeed be independent... Indeed, be independent for you are the difference maker in your life and the entire world.
3. **E**- Evaluate your life & story... Evaluate your story and life from clear eyes and not them eyes of your past and unlearned you.
4. **R** – Realize you make the difference... Realize life is better because you are here and have purpose to fulfill.
5. **C** – Create opportunity through purpose... Create opportunity through purpose the gift in your hand that will bring you before great men and allow you to make wealth.
6. **E** – Evolve into the greatest version of you... Evolve into the greatest version of you that the process of time has allowed you to become who you were born to be.

Fabulously Fierce

I have a gift for you:

https://deborahallen.groovepages.com/free/index

"Finding Your True Passion"

Fabulously Fierce

Dr. Deborah Allen
DEBORAH ALLEN COLLECTION
FABULOUSLY FIERCE EAU DE PARFUM

Indulge in the sultry and seductive aroma of ***Fabulously Fierce Eau De Parfum*** from the Deborah Allen Collection.

This exotic fragrance transports you to a world of sensuality and mystique, with its vibrant blend of top notes including zesty Orange Blossom, juicy Brazilian Cherry, and luscious Fresh Raspberry. The sharp and invigorating notes of Petitgrain, Cardamom and Bergamot add a touch of mystery and intrigue, evoking an air of daring adventure.

As the fragrance settles, the heart notes of Orange Hibiscus, Lily-of-the-Valley, Jasmine, and Sage reveal themselves in a harmonious and intoxicating melody. These floral and herbal notes create a captivating and alluring aura, tempting the senses, and heightening your desire.

Fabulously Fierce

The fragrance lingers with its unforgettable base notes of warm Amber, rich Musk, and smooth Sandalwood. These luxurious and seductive scents create a hypnotic and irresistible trail, leaving you feeling empowered and confident, ready to conquer the world.

Fabulously Fierce Eau De Parfum from the Deborah Allen Collection is the perfect fragrance for those who embrace their sensuality and exude an air of unapologetic confidence. It is a scent that will captivate and enchant those around you, leaving them in awe of your sheer power and magnetism.

Dr. Deborah Allen
DEBORAH ALLEN COLLECTION
FABULOUSLY FIERCE EAU DE PARFUM

Ingredients:

Orange Blossom ~ refers to the fragrant white flowers of the orange tree (Citrus sinensis). These flowers are highly aromatic and are used in various applications, including perfumery, aromatherapy, and culinary arts. Its sweet and floral scent and relaxing properties make it a popular choice in various industries.

Orange Hibiscus ~ is a type of hibiscus plant that produces vibrant, orange-colored flowers. The plant is native to tropical and subtropical regions. In traditional medicine, the orange hibiscus plant has been used to treat various ailments, including high blood pressure, liver disorders, and menstrual cramps.

Brazilian Cherry ~ is a hardwood tree species that is native to the Amazon rainforest and other parts of South America. It is a versatile and valuable tree species with uses in both woodworking and traditional medicine. Its durability and strength make it a popular choice for various applications, while its fruit and medicinal properties add to its cultural and economic significance.

Fresh Raspberries ~ are a delicious and nutritious fruit that are widely enjoyed around the world. They are a member of the rose family. They contain compounds that have anti-inflammatory and antioxidant properties, and they may have potential benefits for cardiovascular health, blood sugar control, and cancer prevention.

Petitgrain ~ is an essential oil that is derived from the leaves and twigs of various citrus trees. Petitgrain has a fresh, floral, and slightly woody scent, and it is often used in perfumery and aromatherapy. It is believed to have calming and balancing effects on the mind and body.

Cardamom ~ is a spice that comes from the seeds of various plants in the ginger family. It is also used in traditional medicine, where it is believed to have digestive, anti-inflammatory, and antimicrobial properties.

Bergamot ~ is a citrus fruit that is commonly used to flavor tea and confectionery. Its essential oil is also used in perfumery and aromatherapy, where it is valued for its refreshing, uplifting scent.

Lily-of-the-Valley ~ is a highly fragrant flowering plant with delicate white, bell-shaped flowers that bloom in the spring. Overall, Lily-of-the-Valley is a beautiful and fragrant plant with cultural and medicinal significance.

Jasmine ~ is a fragrant flowering plant in the olive family. It is native to tropical and subtropical regions of Asia, Europe, and Africa, and is known for its delicate, sweet aroma. The oil is believed to have calming and relaxing effects on the mind and body, and is used to reduce stress, anxiety, and depression.

Amber ~ is a fossilized resin that is derived from the sap of ancient trees. It is typically found in warm, temperate climates around the world, and is known for its warm, rich color and unique beauty. It is believed to have a range of therapeutic properties, including pain relief, anti-inflammatory effects, and the ability to promote healing and detoxification.

Musk ~ is a natural or synthetic substance with a distinctive scent that is often described as earthy, animalistic, or musky. Its unique and distinctive scent has made it a prized ingredient in many cultures, and its potential therapeutic properties continue to be explored and studied.

Sandalwood ~ is a fragrant wood that comes from the Santalum tree, a small tree native to Southeast Asia, Australia, and the South Pacific. Also commonly used in the production of incense and is believed to have spiritual and religious significance in many cultures. It is often used in meditation and prayer and is believed to help promote a sense of calm and relaxation.

Fabulously Fierce

About ~ Dr. Deborah Allen

Finding one's *inner voice,* can be a liberating, awe-inspiring, and transformational experience. Fashioned to help the masses find their "fierce"; is the dynamic professional, Deborah Allen.

Deborah Allen is a 30X best-selling & 15X international best-selling author, speaker, certified life-coach, cleric, and CEO and creative founder of **The Fierce System**; a multifaceted liaison specialty, centered around helping women to both, find and develop, their voice. Having been trained by world-renowned NSA motivational speaker, Mr. Les Brown, Deborah understands the importance of strategy, development, and credible mentorship; traits she seamlessly translates, to her growing clientele.

Deborah's mantra is simple: Her one and only goal is to motivate clients; helping them to create the life, they were meant to live.

Dr. Deborah Allen

Refusing mediocrity on all fronts, Deborah has trailblazed a credible path for those she serves. She has served as Senior Pastor of Lighthouse Apostolic Ministries of God Church, for the last 23 years; and is the Executive Director of the nonprofit organization, L.A.M. Ministries, Inc.

Matching servant leadership with an incredible respect for higher learning, Deborah is a Certified Life Coach; and is a member of the National Speaker Association Speaker (NSA) and a Black Speakers Network (BSN) Speaker. Her conglomerate The Fierce System, is comprised of many platforms, including: Fierce TV, Radio, and blog; as well as Fierce Voices of Destiny Program; where she mentors, develops, and creates strategic alignment between clients, and their true life's calling. She is the Visionary and CEO of Igniting The Flame Publishing, Visionary Coaching & Consulting Group LLC and Deborah Allen Enterprise.

Deborah proudly attests that women are at the heartbeat of all she does, and that it is her desire to see them be strong, fierce, and know, that they can truly achieve their dreams, and walk in purpose. When she is not out helping women to come alive, rebuild, shift and find themselves again; Deborah is a valued asset to her communal body, and a loving member of her family and friendship circles.

Dr. Deborah Allen. Energizer. Organizer. Servant Leader.

Dr. Deborah Allen

Connect with Dr. Apostle Deborah Allen

Igniting The Flame Publishing:

https://www.ignitingtheflamepublishing.com

1st Website: https://deborahallenfierce.com/

2nd Website: https://deborahallenspeaker.com/

Links:
Facebook: https://www.facebook.com/deborahallenfierce

Instagram: https://www.instagram.com/deborahallenfierce/

Twitter: https://twitter.com/deborahallenfierce

Periscope: https://www.pscp.tv/ladydeborahallen/follow

LinkedIn: https://www.linkedin.com/in/prophetessdeborahallen/

YouTube:
https://www.youtube.com/channel/UCTOf0igcAxlVaneH2ZOo_Zg

The Fierce, Ignition & Activation Show/Podcast:
https://envisionedbroadcasting.com/fierceignition

Email: deborahallenfierce@gmail.com

Made in the USA
Columbia, SC
20 March 2023